# Worship Favorites

## CONTENTS

T0081798

### HOW TO USE THE CD ACCOMPANIMENT:

THE CD IS PLAYABLE ON ANY CD PLAYER, AND IS ALSO ENHANCED SO MAC AND PC USERS CAN ADJUST THE RECORDING TO ANY TEMPO WITHOUT CHANGING THE PITCH.

A MELODY CUE APPEARS ON THE RIGHT CHANNEL ONLY. IF YOUR CD PLAYER HAS A BALANCE ADJUSTMENT, YOU CAN ADJUST THE VOLUME OF THE MELODY BY TURNING DOWN THE RIGHT CHANNEL.

ISBN 978-1-4234-9932-9

HAL•LEONARD®
CORPORATION

7777 W. BLUEMOUND RD. P.O. BOX 13819 MILWAUKEE, WI 53213

For all works contained herein:
Unauthorized copying, arranging, adapting, recording, Internet posting, public performance,
or other distribution of the printed or recorded music in this publication is an infringement of copyright.
Infringers are liable under the law.

Visit Hal Leonard Online at
**www.halleonard.com**

# ◆ AGNUS DEI

TENOR SAX

Words and Music by
MICHAEL W. SMITH

Copyright © 1990 Sony/ATV Music Publishing LLC
All Rights Administered by Sony/ATV Music Publishing LLC, 8 Music Square West, Nashville, TN 37203
International Copyright Secured  All Rights Reserved

# ❖ EVERLASTING GOD

TENOR SAX

Words and Music by BRENTON BROWN
and KEN RILEY

**Moderate Rock**

© 2005 THANKYOU MUSIC (PRS)
Admin. Worldwide at EMICMGPUBLISHING.COM excluding Europe which is Admin. at Kingswaysongs
All Rights Reserved   Used by Permission

# ❸ GREAT IS THE LORD

TENOR SAX

Words and Music by MICHAEL W. SMITH
and DEBORAH D. SMITH

© 1982 MEADOWGREEN MUSIC COMPANY (ASCAP)
Admin. at EMICMGPUBLISHING.COM
All Rights Reserved   Used by Permission

# ◆ HE IS EXALTED

TENOR SAX

Words and Music by
TWILA PARIS

© 1985 STRAIGHTWAY MUSIC (ASCAP) and MOUNTAIN SPRING MUSIC (ASCAP)
Admin. at EMICMGPUBLISHING.COM
All Rights Reserved   Used by Permission

# ❺ HERE I AM TO WORSHIP

TENOR SAX

Words and Music by
TIM HUGHES

© 2001 THANKYOU MUSIC (PRS)
Admin. Worldwide at EMICMGPUBLISHING.COM excluding Europe which is Admin. at Kingswaysongs
All Rights Reserved   Used by Permission

# ❻ HOSANNA
## (Praise Is Rising)

TENOR SAX

Words and Music by PAUL BALOCHE
and BRENTON BROWN

**With a driving beat**

© 2006 Integrity's Hosanna! Music/ASCAP (c/o Integrity Media, Inc., 1000 Cody Road, Mobile, AL 36695)
and Thankyou Music/PRS (Admin. Worldwide at EMICMGPublishing.com excluding Europe which is Admin. at Kingswaysongs)
All Rights Reserved   International Copyright Secured   Used by Permission

# 7 HOW MAJESTIC IS YOUR NAME

TENOR SAX

Words and Music by
MICHAEL W. SMITH

© 1981 MEADOWGREEN MUSIC COMPANY (ASCAP)
Admin. at EMICMGPUBLISHING.COM
All Rights Reserved   Used by Permission

# ◆8 IN CHRIST ALONE

TENOR SAX

Words and Music by KEITH GETTY
and STUART TOWNEND

© 2002 THANKYOU MUSIC (PRS)
Admin. Worldwide at EMICMGPUBLISHING.COM excluding Europe which is Admin. at Kingswaysongs
All Rights Reserved   Used by Permission

# ◆9 INDESCRIBABLE

TENOR SAX

Words and Music by LAURA STORY
and JESSE REEVES

© 2004 GLEANING PUBLISHING (ASCAP), WORSHIPTOGETHER.COM SONGS (ASCAP) and sixsteps Music (ASCAP)
Admin. at EMICMGPUBLISHING.COM
All Rights Reserved   Used by Permission

# LEAD ME TO THE CROSS

TENOR SAX

Words and Music by
BROOKE FRASER

© 2006 HILLSONG PUBLISHING (ASCAP)
Admin. in the United States and Canada at EMICMGPUBLISHING.COM
All Rights Reserved   Used by Permission

# MIGHTY TO SAVE

TENOR SAX

Words and Music by BEN FIELDING
and REUBEN MORGAN

© 2006 HILLSONG PUBLISHING (ASCAP)
Admin. in the United States and Canada at EMICMGPUBLISHING.COM
All Rights Reserved    Used by Permission

# THE POWER OF THE CROSS
## (Oh to See the Dawn)

**TENOR SAX**

Words and Music by KEITH GETTY
and STUART TOWNEND

© 2005 THANKYOU MUSIC (PRS)
Admin. Worldwide at EMICMGPUBLISHING.COM excluding Europe which is Admin. at Kingswaysongs
All Rights Reserved   Used by Permission

# ◆13 STILL

TENOR SAX

Words and Music by
REUBEN MORGAN

© 2002 HILLSONG PUBLISHING (ASCAP)
Admin. in the United States and Canada at EMICMGPUBLISHING.COM
All Rights Reserved   Used by Permission

# ◆14 THERE IS A REDEEMER

TENOR SAX

Words and Music by
MELODY GREEN

© 1982 BIRDWING MUSIC (ASCAP), UNIVERSAL MUSIC - MGB SONGS (ASCAP) and EARS TO HEAR MUSIC (ASCAP)
Admin. at EMICMGPUBLISHING.COM
All Rights Reserved   Used by Permission

# THE WONDERFUL CROSS

TENOR SAX

Words and Music by JESSE REEVES,
CHRIS TOMLIN and J. D. WALT

© 2000 WORSHIPTOGETHER.COM SONGS (ASCAP) and sixsteps Music (ASCAP)
Admin. at EMICMGPUBLISHING.COM
All Rights Reserved   Used by Permission